Straight to the Source

Newspapers

John Hamilton

ABDO
Publishing Company

visit us at

www.abdopub.com

Published by ABDO Publishing Company, 4940 Viking Drive, Edina, Minnesota 55435.
Copyright © 2005 by Abdo Consulting Group, Inc. International copyrights reserved in all
countries. No part of this book may be reproduced in any form without written permission from
the publisher. The Checkerboard Library™ is a trademark and logo of ABDO Publishing
Company.

Printed in the United States.

Cover Photo: Corbis
Interior Photos: Corbis pp. 1, 5, 8, 9, 11, 13, 14, 15, 16, 18-19, 21, 22, 25, 26, 28;
    Getty Images p. 15; North Wind p. 7

Series Coordinator: Stephanie Hedlund
Editors: Stephanie Hedlund, Kristin Van Cleaf
Art Direction: Neil Klinepier

Library of Congress Cataloging-in-Publication Data

Hamilton, John, 1959-
    Newspapers / John Hamilton.
       p. cm. -- (Straight to the source)
    Includes index.
    Summary: A look at the history of newspapers, famous news agencies and people, parts of a
typical newspaper, how newspapers are made and how they can be used to research a report.
    ISBN 1-59197-547-6
    1. Newspapers--Juvenile literature. [1. Newspapers. 2. Research--Methodology.] I. Title.

PN4776.H36 2004
070.1'72--dc22
                                                                    2003057884

Contents

Newspapers 4
The New News 6
Types of Papers 10
Newsgathering 12
Common Parts 16
Making Money 20
The Newsroom 22
Sent to Press 24
Article Search 26
Citing Papers 28
Glossary 30
Saying It 31
Web Sites 31
Index 32

Newspapers

When you read a newspaper, you learn about current events. Newspapers tell you what is happening around the world. They also keep you in touch with news in your own neighborhood.

News is information about something that has just happened or is about to happen. Obviously, not everything is reported. Newspaper editors print stories they think people will want to read.

You can learn more from newspapers than just news. Papers also provide practical information such as weather forecasts, financial reports, and television schedules. Some people read the paper to find sports scores or to be entertained.

Newspapers are more up-to-date than books. They have more variety than magazines. And, they provide more details than television. So, newspapers are a useful part of the research process.

Journalist John Bogart said in 1918, "When a dog bites a man, that is not news, because it happens so often. But if a man bites a dog, that is news."

The New News

Newspapers have only been around for a few hundred years. Before newspapers, people received the day's news by word of mouth. **Town criers** walked through villages and announced local news such as births, deaths, and weddings.

In ancient Rome, news was posted throughout the city in written notes. These notes were called *Acta Diurna*, or "Daily Events." *Acta Diurna* announced social events and politics. In China, printed newspapers called *paos* reported court affairs.

Over time, several inventions made printing easier. One was developed in the 1450s by German printer Johannes Gutenberg. He developed a press that used **movable type**, which made printing copies of a **manuscript** easier.

Pamphlets and newsletters began appearing in Europe around 1500. As **literacy** grew, people wanted more news. In the 1600s, Germany and Japan printed news on one side of a sheet of paper. These were called fly sheets.

Fly sheets led to the next form of paper. In 1620, the Dutch published *corantos*, meaning "currents of news." These commercial bulletins provided news from all over Europe.

Johannes Gutenberg was a goldsmith. His work with metals led to movable type.

In 1665, the *Oxford Gazette* became England's first true newspaper. In North America, the first newspaper was published in 1690 in Boston, Massachusetts. It was called *Publick Occurrences, Both Foreign and Domestick*.

Throughout the 1700s, more newspapers were established in America. However, many had short **life spans**. Printing costs and government **censorship** caused many newspapers to go out of business.

In 1791, the U.S. Constitution was amended to include the Bill of Rights. It contained the First Amendment, which **guaranteed** freedom of the press. More newspapers developed in the United States at this time.

Freedom of the Press

In many countries, the government controls the news that is released. But in the United States, newspapers are mostly free to report whatever they want about the government. This is because the First Amendment of the U.S. Constitution guarantees freedom of the press.

Throughout history, the First Amendment has been challenged. One of the most famous cases occurred in New York. In 1735, New York's governor jailed John Peter Zenger. Zenger had printed articles in the **New York Weekly Journal** *that the governor didn't like. At his trial, Zenger was found innocent. The American public began to see the importance of having a free press.*

Literacy began to spread during the 1800s. Papers were sold for about six cents then. This was expensive for the average person. So, Benjamin Day's *Sun* and other papers began selling their **editions** for a penny. This led to the "penny press" period from 1830 to 1860.

More than 6.5 million people read USA Today every day!

In the late 1800s, the country was expanding. Soon, rail lines and postal routes were transporting newspapers across the country. By 1914, there were more than 15,000 newspapers in the United States.

After **World War II**, many newspapers closed or **merged** with others. But today, nearly every city has a daily newspaper. Many small towns also have weekly papers. There are also three national papers, the *Wall Street Journal*, *USA Today*, and the *New York Times*.

Types of Papers

Many advancements have been made in the newspaper industry. Today, most papers have an **edition** that can be read on the Internet. But, printed newspapers are still read by millions of people every day.

Newspapers are printed on a type of paper called newsprint. In the United States, standard-sized newspapers measure about 15 by 23 inches (38 by 58 cm). Tabloid newspapers are slightly smaller, measuring about 11 by 15 inches (28 by 38 cm).

There are several types of newspapers. Dailies are published every day. They cover world, national, state, and local news. They report on science, business, the environment, and the arts.

EXTRA!

U.S. Papers

There are 50,000 newspapers worldwide. At least one-third are U.S. papers. In the United States there are 1,800 dailies and 7,600 weeklies. There are also 6,000 free newspapers and 2,000 college papers printed every year.

*The term **tabloid** has two meanings. One refers to the size of paper. The other meaning reflects a paper's violent, scandalous content. So, there can be serious newspapers that are tabloids.*

Another type of paper is the weekly. Weeklies usually cover a smaller area than dailies. In small towns, there is great interest in local events such as weddings, births, and funerals. Local businesses and small-town politics are also widely covered.

Some papers publish news about special interests. For example, many cover certain industries. Tabloids report celebrity news and gossip. Other papers provide news about **ethnic** groups or are printed in a foreign language. Many schools publish their own newspapers.

Newsgathering

Newspapers obtain stories in two ways. One way is by sending out their own reporters. Another is by using news agencies. News agencies write and sell stories to anyone who needs news. They make it easier for small papers to print news from around the world.

The first news agency started in 1848. That year, six New York papers began working together to gather and share news. They called their organization the New York Associated Press. In 1922, the company became the Associated Press (AP).

Today, 1,550 U.S. newspapers and 5,000 radio and television stations use the AP. It has more than 8,500 news **subscribers** in 112 countries. More than 1 billion people read or hear an AP news story every day.

During its early years, the AP restricted who could buy its stories. Publisher E.W. Scripps thought that was wrong. In 1907, he started United Press Associations (UP). Its stories were available to anyone.

Opposite page: *Reporters for UPI, such as Charlie McCarty, were called Unipressers. Other famous Unipressers include Walter Cronkite, Helen Thomas, and Raymond Clapper.*

EXTRA!

Reuter's News Agency

In 1851, Paul Julius Reuter started Reuter's News Agency. Reuter was a German immigrant who sent stock market quotations between London and Paris. The agency expanded its service to other European countries. Today, it sells general and economic news stories all over the world. Reuter's is located in Great Britain.

In 1958, UP **merged** with William Randolph Hearst's International News Service. This merger formed United Press International (UPI). Today, UPI's headquarters is in Washington, D.C. It has offices all over the world.

Famous People

E.W. Scripps

Joseph Pulitzer came to the United States from Hungary in 1864. He started in journalism by working at the St. Louis Post-Dispatch. In 1883, he bought the New York World. Pulitzer's papers practiced yellow journalism, which exaggerated the news or was sometimes false. They also competed with William Randolph Hearst's papers. Pulitzer's will allotted money to start Columbia University's School of Journalism and the Pulitzer Prize. Each year the Pulitzer Prize honors the best journalists worldwide.

E.W. Scripps started his career working at the Detroit Evening News in 1872. Six years later, he started the Cleveland Penny Press. Scripps soon bought several other papers. In 1894, he set up a chain of papers called the Scripps-McRae League of Newspapers. In 1907, Scripps helped start the United Press Associations (UP) news agency.

Joseph Pulitzer

William Randolph Hearst

In 1887, William Randolph Hearst started running the San Francisco Examiner. Hearst wanted to make the Examiner popular. He hired the best writers, including Ambrose Bierce and Winifred Black. He also practiced yellow journalism. Hearst became very powerful in journalism and in politics. At the height of his power, he owned 28 newspapers. He also owned several magazines, radio stations, and movie companies.

Katharine Graham took over her family's newspaper, the Washington Post, in 1963. Under her leadership, the Washington Post became known for its excellent investigative journalism. For example, in 1972 the newspaper published a series of articles about the Watergate scandal. This led to the resignation of President Richard Nixon. In 1998, Graham won the Pulitzer Prize for her autobiography, Personal History.

Katharine Graham

Common Parts

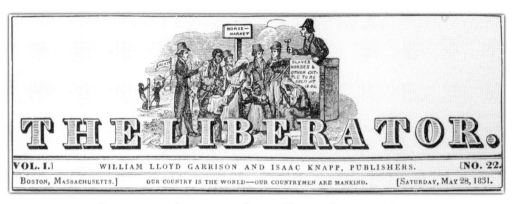

Some nameplates contain an illustration or a slogan.

Though every newspaper looks different, some elements are common to all papers. One common element is the nameplate, or flag. It is on the front page of a newspaper. The nameplate contains the paper's name, price, date, and **edition**.

Another element in all newspapers is the masthead. It is found inside a newspaper, usually on the editorial page. The masthead provides the publisher information. This includes the paper's address and phone numbers, as well as the names of executives and editors.

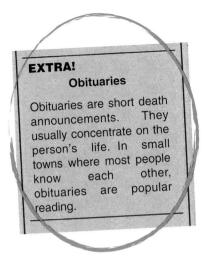

All newspapers are organized in similar ways. For example, several columns are laid out on each page. Narrow columns are easier for the eye to follow. So, newspapers usually have four to nine columns on a page.

Newspaper columns are used to organize articles. An article can be about almost any subject. Some stories are simple news items that may run in one column. Others are thousands of words long. Important stories might take up all nine columns or run over a number of days.

This paper has six columns of type.

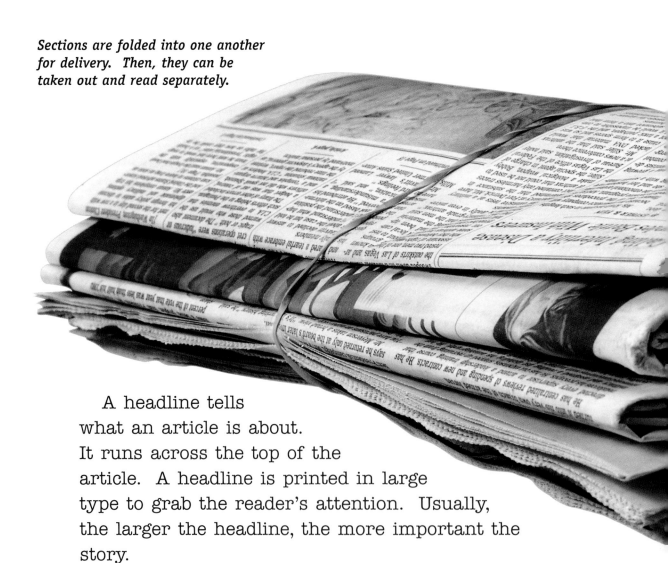

A headline tells what an article is about. It runs across the top of the article. A headline is printed in large type to grab the reader's attention. Usually, the larger the headline, the more important the story.

Under the headline is the byline. This element tells who wrote the article. Sometimes newspapers use stories written by reporters from other papers or news agencies. This information is also found in the byline.

Large newspapers often organize their articles into sections. Most papers include news, opinion, sports, entertainment, and classified sections. Each section may have a different number of pages depending on the amount of news to be reported.

Newspapers print opinions on an editorial page. There, opinions about politics or pressing matters of the day appear. The opinion section may also contain editorial cartoons and letters to the editor.

Making Money

Another common element in all newspapers is advertising. Approximately 75 percent of a paper's income is from advertising. The other 25 percent comes from **subscriptions** and newsstand sales. So, advertising keeps a newspaper running.

Newspapers run two types of ads. Classified ads are also known as want ads. They are usually small, text-only offers to buy and sell products. Often these products are used goods. Classified ads frequently have their own section in the paper.

Display ads show products and services, often with pictures. Newspapers make the most money from these ads. So, most papers try to fill 60 percent of their space with display ads. The remaining space is devoted to news.

Sunday **editions** of newspapers carry a large number of ads. Some display ads take up a whole page. Others appear as **inserts**.

Want ads may list items that are for sale or jobs that are available.

The Newsroom

The newsroom is where fast-breaking reports are written and edited. These reports, called spot news, might include stories about fires, murders, or other timely events.

Once all the elements are determined, it is time to put a newspaper together. Many people work together to get a paper ready for press.

The publisher is the highest-ranking person at a newspaper. Because he or she can't do everything alone, a publisher gets help from department heads. Typical departments include editorial, advertising, marketing, production, and circulation.

Reporters are also important employees. They gather news by interviewing people in person or over the phone. They also research subjects in libraries and government records. Then, they write their stories.

Next, editors take the stories from reporters and make sure they are factual. Proper grammar and style must be used. Editors have a responsibility to make sure each story is correct.

There are many kinds of editors. Usually a single editor leads a section of the paper. Working under the editor are various assistant editors and copy editors who get the stories ready to print.

While a reporter and editor are working on a story, a newspaper's photojournalist is finding images for it. Photojournalists take photos of many things, including fires, crime scenes, and portraits. In recent years, photographers have started using **digital** cameras.

Sent to Press

After stories have been written and edited, they are ready for page layout. First, the advertising department places its ads on blank newspaper pages called dummies. The news hole, or remaining space, is then filled with stories and photos.

During this process, newspaper designers try to lay out the stories so that they will attract readers. Most newspapers today use computer programs to arrange the text and photos on the page. And, it all has to be done under constant **deadline** pressure.

Once all the pages have been laid out and approved, the **digital** files are sent to press. There, the newspaper is printed. Almost every newspaper uses a process called offset lithography.

EXTRA!
Offset Lithography

In offset lithography, large cylinders hold curved printing plates. The plates are first coated with ink. Then, they copy an image of the newspaper to rubber "blanket" cylinders. The blanket cylinders then transfer the ink onto long rolls of newsprint. The newsprint is moving at high speeds, so many copies of the paper are printed quickly.

After the paper is printed, it is cut, folded, and stacked into piles. Then, conveyor belts take the stacks to the circulation department.

In the circulation department, some papers are addressed and mailed. Fleets of trucks deliver others directly to homes or offices. A smaller number is sold at stores or on newsstands. Some newspapers are also sold in machines at airports or bus stations.

Newspapers are printed on large rolls of paper called webs.

Article Search

Newspapers are good resources to use when writing research papers. They are published often, so they provide the most current news. And, their articles contain basic information without too many confusing details.

Newspapers inform and entertain. They are also a good place to search for basic information.

Newspapers are often thrown away after they are read. So to find newspaper articles, it is best to visit a library. Libraries have large computer **databases** of news articles.

Libraries also have newspaper indexes. These indexes can be in a print or online format. They give short summaries of news stories. Then they provide the date, section, page, and column the story is on.

Most libraries will have access to the full text of any newspaper article. It may be found in print, on **microfiche**, or on a computer. A librarian can help you find an article in any of these formats.

Using the Newspaper

To find information in a newspaper, look at the front page. There, several items will lead you to information within the paper.

◆ *Teasers - the top of the front page promotes the biggest stories of the issue and their page numbers.*

◆ *Index - a box that gives the section and page number of regular items.*

◆ *Refer - a line or paragraph set off by graphics that refers to a related story that is found elsewhere in the paper.*

◆ *Jump line - a line at the end of a story that tells what page it continues on.*

Citing Papers

When evaluating newspapers, ask who, what, when, where, and why.

Newspapers try to be very **accurate** with their information. But many newspapers are published every day. Tight **deadlines** mean coverage is less in-depth. For this reason, newspapers are not as reliable as other sources, such as books.

Be careful when using a newspaper to write a research paper. **Evaluate** any information you find in a newspaper article. If you find a statement about your topic, make sure it is supported by hard facts. And, try to find the same fact in more than one article.

When writing your report, put the information in your own words. Copying someone else's work is called **plagiarism**. You will get in trouble at school for plagiarizing. Reporters get fired for doing it!

There are two ways to avoid plagiarism. First, summarize the article in your own words. This is called paraphrasing. Second, cite your sources by including which newspaper you got the information from.

Newspapers are a great way to stay informed. People depend on newspapers to tell them about current events. If you have questions on how to use a newspaper, ask your teacher or librarian for help.

EXTRA!

MLA Citation

There are several ways to cite sources. One of the most common is Modern Language Association (MLA) style.

MLA's style for newspaper citation includes several pieces of information. First, cite the author's name. Next, include the title of the article in quotation marks. Then, give the underlined title of the newspaper, the date of publication, and the section and page number.

If the city of the newspaper is not in its name, put it in brackets after the name of the paper. If an edition is listed on the nameplate, put a comma after the date and cite the edition.

Harlow, Tim. "Step right up." Star Tribune [Minneapolis] 20 June 2003, metro ed.: E18.

Glossary

accurate - free of errors.

censor - to suppress or remove material that is considered offensive.

database - a large collection of information.

deadline - a set time before copy has to be finished.

digital - numeric data that can be read by computer.

edition - an issue of a publication.

ethnic - of or having to do with a group of people who have the same race, nationality, or culture.

evaluate - to determine the meaning or importance of something.

guarantee - to make sure or certain.

insert - an extra section, such as advertisements, placed in a paper.

life span - the length of time an organization, paper, or individual exists.

literacy - the state of being able to read and write.

manuscript - a book or article written by hand or typed before being published.

merge - to combine two or more businesses into one business.

microfiche - a sheet of film that contains reduced images of printed materials such as magazines. Microfiche must be read on a special machine that magnifies the images.

movable type - a rectangular block that contains a letter or symbol for printing. It can be moved or rearranged to produce different pages.

pamphlet - a printed publication without a cover.

plagiarism - using someone else's words or ideas without giving him or her credit.

subscribe - to agree to receive and pay for a publication.

town crier - a town officer who makes announcements.

World War II - from 1939 to 1945, fought in Europe, Asia, and Africa. Great Britain, France, the United States, the Soviet Union, and their allies were on one side. Germany, Italy, Japan, and their allies were on the other side.

editorial - eh-duh-TAWR-ee-uhl

pamphlet - PAMP-fluht

plagiarism - PLAY-juh-rih-zuhm

subscription - suhb-SKRIHP-shuhn

tabloid - TA-bloyd

Web Sites

To learn more about newspapers, visit ABDO Publishing Company on the World Wide Web at **www.abdopub.com**. Web sites about newspapers are featured on our Book Links page. These links are routinely monitored and updated to provide the most current information available.

Index

A
advertising 20, 23, 24
articles 4, 12, 17, 18, 19, 23, 24, 26, 27, 28, 29

B
Bill of Rights 8
Boston, Massachusetts 8
byline 18, 19

C
China 6
columns 17, 27
Constitution, U.S. 8

D
Day, Benjamin 9
departments 23, 24, 25

E
editorial page 16, 19
England 8
Europe 6, 7
evaluation 28

F
First Amendment 8

G
Germany 6
Gutenberg, Johannes 6

H
headline 18
Hearst, William Randolph 13

I
Internet 10, 27

J
Japan 6

L
librarian 27, 29
library 23, 27

M
masthead 16

N
nameplate 16
news agencies 12, 13, 19
North America 8

P
paraphrase 29
"penny press" period 9
plagiarism 28, 29
printing 6, 24, 25

R
research papers 26, 28, 29
Rome 6

S
Scripps, E.W. 12
sections 19, 20, 23, 27
staff 4, 12, 16, 19, 22, 23, 24, 29

T
types of newspapers 6, 7, 8, 9, 10, 11

U
United States 8, 9, 10, 12

W
Washington, D.C. 13
World War II 9